The STORY of JOSEPH

By James Edson White
Pioneer Series

VOL. III

THE UPWARD WAY
P.O. Box 9009
Nampa, Idaho 83652
Printed in the U.S.A.

THE PIONEER SERIES

I Christ, Our Savior
II Best Stories from the Best Book
III The Story of Joseph
IV Scrapbook Stories

ISBN-0-945460-07-4

ART DIRECTION / COVER DESIGN: ED GUTHERO
COVER ILLUSTRATION: LARS JUSTINEN

COPYRIGHTED, 1902, By J. E. WHITE.

ALL RIGHTS RESERVED.

© 1989 by the Upward Way

The Upward Way
P.O. Box 9009 Nampa, Idaho 83652

For more information on this book and other titles in the Pioneer Series call 1-800-FOR-BOOK.

Joseph's Ancestors.

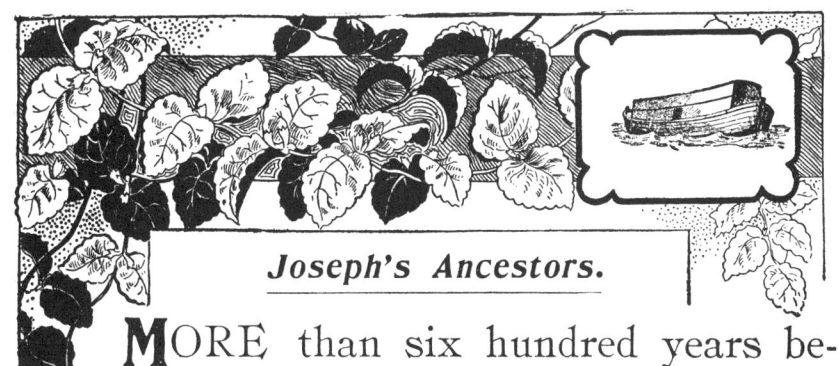

MORE than six hundred years before Joseph was born, the people on earth had become very wicked.

They forgot about the true God of heaven, and worshiped idols made of wood and stone.

At last God could bear with them no longer. So He sent a flood of waters upon the earth and destroyed them.

But Noah and his family were true to God, so the Lord saved them, and some of all kinds of beasts and birds, in a great boat called the ark.

The Lord led the beasts and birds into the ark. It must have been a beautiful sight to see them come, "two and two," without any one to lead them, and take their places in the ark.

When all were in place, the Lord shut the door of the ark. Then there was an awful storm that lasted forty days. And the whole earth was covered with water.

When the waters of the flood went down, Noah came out of the ark. And he took some of the best of the beasts that had been saved in the ark, and slew them, and burned them as a sacrifice to God.

This offering pleased the Lord, for Noah had only a very few beasts. All that had not gone into the ark were dead.

And the Lord put the rainbow in the clouds

NOAH'S SACRIFICE

JOSEPH'S ANCESTORS.   5

as a sign that He would never again destroy the world by a flood.

After the flood the family of Noah increased very rapidly and spread abroad in the earth.

They soon forgot God, and began to worhip idols as people did before the flood.

MOLOCH, THE HEATHEN GOD OF FIRE.

This idol was made of metal, hollow, with a furnace for fire inside. It was heated until the hollow arms were very hot, and then infants were placed in its arms and roasted as an awful sacrifice to this idol. Heathen worship is often very cruel, but the worship of the true God is gentle and full of love.

THE TOWER OF BABEL.
"And the people were scattered."

Then they built a great tower, called the tower of Babel. They thought they would build it so high that if another flood should come, they could climb to the top of it and be saved.

But the Lord was not pleased with this rebellious work, and so He changed their language, so that some spoke one language and some another.

After that no one could understand what the others said to him, and so they could not work together. Hence the work ceased and the people were scattered.

JOSEPH'S ANCESTORS.

The patriarch Abraham was born only two years after the death of Noah. He was true to God, and did not worship idols like the wicked people around him.

When Abraham was seventy-five years old, the Lord came to him, and told him to leave his home and the idolatrous people who lived near him, and go into another land of which He would tell him.

The Lord also told Abraham that his children should become a great nation, and that He would give them the land of Canaan as their home. So he journeyed toward Canaan.

ABRAHAM JOURNEYING FROM HIS HOME TO CANAAN.

But the most wonderful promise made to Abraham was that, after hundreds of years, Christ, the Saviour of the world, would come in the line of his family.

Abraham had a son named Isaac. He obeyed his father in all things, and was true to God, like his father.

Isaac had two sons, whose names were Jacob and Esau. Jacob was a faithful shepherd, and took care of his father's flocks; while Esau was a hunter. Jacob loved and served the God of his father, but Esau did not obey the Lord.

These brothers did not agree, and Jacob had to go far from home, where he lived many years. When he came back, he had twelve sons.

Ten of these sons were not good men. They did not obey their father, but took their own way, and were very hard hearted.

But the two younger sons, Joseph and Benjamin, loved their father, and were obedient to him.

Joseph's Dreams.

JACOB loved Joseph more than all his other sons, because he was kind and obedient. To show his love, he made Joseph a beautiful coat of many colors. But his brothers hated him, because they saw that their father loved him more than he did them.

The Lord had a great work for Joseph to do. He gave him two wonderful dreams, which came true many years after.

In the first dream, Joseph saw himself and his eleven brothers in the field

JOSEPH'S DREAM OF THE SHEAVES.

THE STORY OF JOSEPH.

binding grain into bundles, or sheaves.

And his sheaf arose and stood upright, and his brothers' sheaves bowed down to his sheaf.

It is probable that Joseph did not know what his dream meant. Had he known, he would not have told it to his brothers.

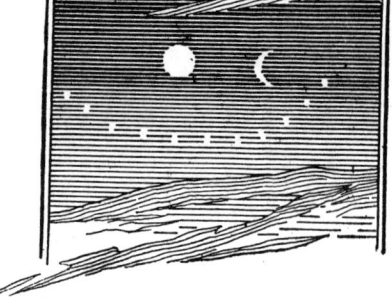

When he did tell it to them, they hated him more than ever, and asked if he thought he would rule them.

JOSEPH'S DREAM OF SUN, MOON, AND STARS.

Some time after this, Joseph dreamed that the sun, moon, and eleven stars bowed down to him. And he told this dream also.

And his father said, "Shall I, and thy

JOSEPH'S DREAMS.

mother, and thy brethren indeed come to bow down ourselves to thee to the earth?"

But years afterward, when the famine came, his father, his brothers, and their families had to depend on Joseph in Egypt for all the food which they ate.

JOSEPH TELLING HIS DREAMS TO HIS BROTHERS.

Joseph Sold as a Slave.

JOSEPH'S brothers were shepherds, and cared for their father's sheep. Sometimes they were compelled to go far away from home to find grass, for Jacob had large flocks.

One day Jacob sent Joseph to find his brothers. They had wandered many miles away in search of pasture, and he wanted to know if they were well.

Joseph had a hard time in finding them, for they had gone fifteen miles from the place where their father thought they were.

When they saw him coming, these wicked brothers said, "Behold, this dreamer cometh. Let us slay him, and cast him

JOSEPH SOLD AS A SLAVE.

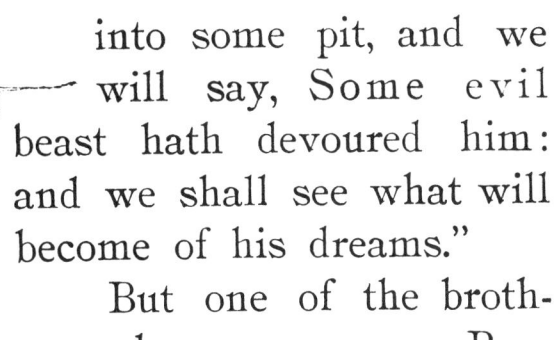

into some pit, and we will say, Some evil beast hath devoured him: and we shall see what will become of his dreams."

But one of the brothers, whose name was Reuben, was not so hard hearted as the others. He would not consent to have Joseph killed. He told them it

WHERE ARE THEY? would be better to cast him alive into a pit than to kill him.

Reuben intended to return to the pit after the others had gone away, and draw his brother out, and send him home to his father.

So when Joseph came up to them, instead of speaking kindly to him, and offering him food, for he was very tired and hungry, his brothers took hold of him roughly, tore off his beautiful coat, and then cast him alive into a deep pit.

Joseph Sold to the Ishmaelites.

JOSEPH SOLD AS A SLAVE.

Joseph loved his brothers, and appealed to each one to save him from the pit, but they would not.

It was not very long until a band of Ishmaelites came along on their way to Egypt, and the brothers drew Joseph out of the pit and sold him to them to be a slave.

Reuben was absent when Joseph was sold. He was very

TAKING JOSEPH OUT OF THE PIT.

sorry when he came to take Joseph out of the pit, and saw he was not there. He tore his coat, and said, "The child is not; and I, whither shall I go?"

Showing Joseph's bloody Coat to Jacob.

JOSEPH SOLD AS A SLAVE.

Then they all began to think of their father, and what they should tell him. So they killed a young goat from the flock, and then dipped the coat in its blood.

Then they took the coat to their father, and told him a lie. They said they had found the coat all covered with blood, and brought it to

REUBEN AT THE PIT.

him to know if it was Joseph's coat. So one sin often leads to another.

Jacob knew the coat as soon as he saw it, and said, "It is my son's coat; an evil beast hath devoured him; Joseph is without doubt rent in pieces." And Jacob mourned for his son Joseph many days.

Joseph in Egypt.

THE Ishmaelites, who bought Joseph, took him to Egypt. There they sold him to Potiphar, who was a very rich man, and captain of the king's guard.

The Lord blessed Joseph, and Potiphar soon saw that whatever he did prospered. So he made him steward of all that he had.

But God had a higher place for Joseph, and he must reach it through affliction. In all his troubles it was the Lord who was giving Joseph just the training he needed to fit him for the great work before him.

While living in the house of Potiphar, Joseph met the most learned men of Egypt, and from them gained knowledge that helped to fit him to rule in the land when he was called to do so.

Potiphar's wife was a wicked woman, and told a falsehood about Joseph. Then Potiphar had Joseph cast into prison, where he remained for several years.

But even in prison "the Lord was with Joseph, and showed him mercy, and gave him favor in the sight of the keeper of the prison."

The jailor soon saw that Joseph could be trusted, so he gave him charge of the prison and all the prisoners.

Now the king's chief butler and chief baker had displeased him, and he cast them into the prison where Joseph was. And they were both placed under his special care.

One morning, when Joseph came to see these men, he found them looking very sad. And he asked them, "Wherefore look ye so sadly to-day?"

20   THE STORY OF JOSEPH.

And they answered him, "We have dreamed a dream, and there is no interpreter of it."

JOSEPH INTERPRETING THE DREAMS OF THE BUTLER AND BAKER.

Joseph said, "Do not interpretations belong to God?" Then he asked them to tell their dreams to him.

Then the chief butler said that in his dream, a grape vine with three branches was before him. And the vine bore fruit, and he took the grapes, and pressed them into Pharaoh's cup for him to drink.

JOSEPH IN EGYPT.

The Lord gave to Joseph the meaning of the dream; so he told the chief butler that the three branches in his dream were three days, and that in three days king Pharaoh would take him out of prison, and restore him to his position as chief butler.

DREAM OF THE CHIEF BUTLER.

Joseph told the butler the story of his own wrongs. He asked the butler to tell his story to the king, and to do all he could to get him out of prison.

But the butler was like many other people who forget those who have been their friends in trouble. When he came out of prison, he forgot all about Joseph.

When the chief baker saw that the dream of the chief butler was good, he was encouraged to tell his dream also.

THE STORY OF JOSEPH.

He dreamed that he had three white baskets on his head, one above the other. In the top basket were all kinds of baked food for the king. And the birds came and ate the food from the top basket.

Joseph told him that the three baskets meant three days, and that in three days Pharaoh would take him from prison, and hang him on a tree, and the birds would eat his flesh.

Both of these dreams came true according to the interpretation that Joseph had given.

THE BAKER'S DREAM.

Although the chief butler forgot about Joseph as soon as he was taken out of prison, the Lord did not forget him, for He had a great work for him to do.

PHARAOHS DREAM

Pharaoh's Dreams.

ABOUT two years after these events, king Pharaoh himself had two dreams. In these dreams he was standing by the river Nile, which the Egyptians worship as one of their gods.

As he looked he saw seven well-fed cattle come up out of the river. And they came up on the bank of the river, and began to eat the grass that grew there.

Afterward he saw seven lean and ill-

THE SEVEN LEAN CATTLE.

JOSEPH, 24.

PHARAOH'S DREAMS.

looking cattle come up out of the river. And the lean cattle ate up the fat cattle. But after they had eaten them the lean cattle were no fatter than before.

After this dream Pharaoh awoke, and then he slept and dreamed again. He saw seven plump and good ears of corn grow on one stalk.

GOOD EARS

BAD EARS

After they had grown, seven blasted and empty ears grew up beside the good ears. And the seven bad ears ate up the seven good ears.

THE SEVEN FAT CATTLE.

THE STORY OF JOSEPH.

These dreams troubled the king very much. So he called in the magicians and wise men of Egypt, and told them the dreams.

These men claimed to have wisdom to interpret dreams, but they were not able to tell the king the meaning of his dreams. God only can reveal such secrets. Men can only pretend to explain them.

THE BUTLER TELLS THE KING ABOUT JOSEPH.

Then the chief butler remembered Joseph. He said, "I do remember my faults this day." He then told the king about Joseph in prison, and how he had interpreted his dream,

PHARAOH'S DREAMS.

and that of the chief baker, and how the interpretation had come true.

Then Pharaoh sent and had Joseph brought to him from the prison. And the king said to him:

"I have dreamed a dream, and there is none that can interpret it; and I have heard say of thee, that thou canst understand a dream to interpret it."

And Joseph answered, "It is not in me; God shall give Pharaoh an answer of peace."

Then the king told his dreams. And Joseph told Pharaoh that both dreams meant the same thing. The seven good cattle, and the seven good ears of corn, meant seven years of plenty in the land.

But the seven lean cattle, and the seven blasted and empty ears of corn, meant seven years of famine that should follow the seven years of plenty.

Joseph then advised Pharaoh to gather all the grain that could be spared during

INTERPRETING PHARAOHS DREAM

the seven years of plenty, and store it up for food to last during the seven years of famine.

He also advised Pharaoh to select a wise and good man to have charge of this work, so that it should be done properly.

Pharaoh was pleased with this advice, and said to Joseph, "Forasmuch as God hath showed thee all this, there is none so discreet and wise as thou art."

And the king made Joseph next to him the highest ruler in all the land of Egypt. He was also given full charge of gathering and storing the grain which was to keep the people alive during the seven years of famine.

In those days it was the custom for the king to wear a seal ring on his hand, with which he signed all decrees. Pharaoh took his seal ring off his hand and gave it to Joseph, and put a royal chain of gold about his neck.

"And he made him ride in the second chariot which he had; and they cried before him, Bow the knee: and he made him ruler over all the land of Egypt."

JOSEPH IN THE SECOND CHARIOT OF EGYPT.

And Pharaoh said unto Joseph, "I am Pharaoh, and without thee shall no man lift up his hand or foot in all the land of Egypt."

Joseph then built storehouses and barns in all the land, and in them was stored grain in great quantity. So much was gathered that they stopped counting it, "for it was without number."

Joseph Meets His Brethren.

WHEN the seven years of plenty were ended, the long famine began, just as Joseph had said. And when the corn that the people had saved for themselves was gone, they came to him for bread. And he opened the public storehouses, and sold grain to them.

Now the famine was in all lands, but in Egypt alone had they stored grain during the years of plenty. And all countries came to Egypt to buy from Joseph.

Thus all the world learned how the God of Joseph had warned Egypt that the famine was coming. By this all nations were taught lessons about the true God which they would never forget.

THE STORY OF JOSEPH.

The store of grain in Egypt was so great that it supplied the people of all lands during the seven long years of famine. So, although Joseph had come to Egypt as a slave, all nations had now to depend on him for the food they ate.

Truly God had blessed and honored Joseph for his faith, trust, and obedience.

JACOB SENDING HIS SONS TO EGYPT TO BUY CORN.

When food began to be scarce in Jacob's family, he said to his sons, "I have heard that there is corn in Egypt; get you down thither, and buy for us from thence; that we may live and not die."

So Joseph's ten brothers went down

JOSEPH MEETS HIS BRETHREN.

JOSEPH'S BRETHREN JOURNEYING TO EGYPT.

to Egypt to buy grain. But Benjamin did not go with them, for his father feared that some evil might befall him.

When these brothers came to Joseph, who was now governor of all Egypt, they "bowed down themselves before him with their faces to the earth."

Joseph knew his brothers as soon as he saw them, but they did not know him. How could they think that the great governor of Egypt was the poor lad they had sold to the Ishmaelites so many years before?

As Joseph saw them bowing before him, he remembered his dream of the

34 THE STORY OF JOSEPH.

sheaves in the field. As their sheaves bowed to his sheaf, so were his brothers now bowing to him.

Although Joseph loved his brethren, he remembered how cruel and wicked they had been when he was with them,

SO HE SAID, "YE ARE SPIES."

and he decided to test them to see if they had changed.

So he said, "Ye are spies; to see the nakedness of the land are ye come."

They answered, "Nay, my lord, but to buy food are thy servants come."

JOSEPH MEETS HIS BRETHREN.

Again Joseph accused them of being spies. But the ten brothers answered that they all belonged to a family of twelve brothers. The youngest was at home with their father, and one was dead.

They had never heard from Joseph after they had sold him to the Ishmaelites, and did not suppose he was alive.

Joseph still called them spies. He told them he would not let them go until they brought their youngest brother. If they would bring him, he would believe their story.

He said that one could return and get Benjamin, and the rest would be kept in prison until Benjamin should return with him.

During the years since Joseph had been betrayed and sold, these brothers had changed very much. They were now true to one another, and loved and honored their father.

They feared that if they brought

MONEY IN THE SACKS

Benjamin into Egypt, some harm would come to him. So they refused to go for Benjamin, and decided to all stay and suffer together.

They were therefore all cast into prison, and were kept there three days. Then Joseph sent for them, and had them brought before him.

He told them that he feared God, and wanted to do right by them. He proposed that nine of the brothers go back to their father with the food, and that one remain in prison until they returned with Benjamin. To this they all agreed.

They did not suppose that Joseph, the governor, understood their language, so they talked freely among themselves. They said that they were now being punished for their cruelty to Joseph many years before.

How Joseph longed to tell them who he was, but he wanted to be sure that they had really repented and were changed.

THE STORY OF JOSEPH.

So Joseph took Simeon, and bound him, and sent him to prison. Simeon was chosen because he had been the most guilty in selling Joseph to the Ishmaelites.

Then Joseph commanded that his brothers' sacks should be filled with corn, and they be allowed to go home. He also told his servants to put into the sacks the money that each one had paid for the grain.

SIMEON IN PRISON.

Afterward, when they opened their sacks, and the money was found in them, they were again very much frightened.

"And they came to Jacob their father unto the land of Canaan, and told him all that befell unto them."

Second Journey to Egypt.

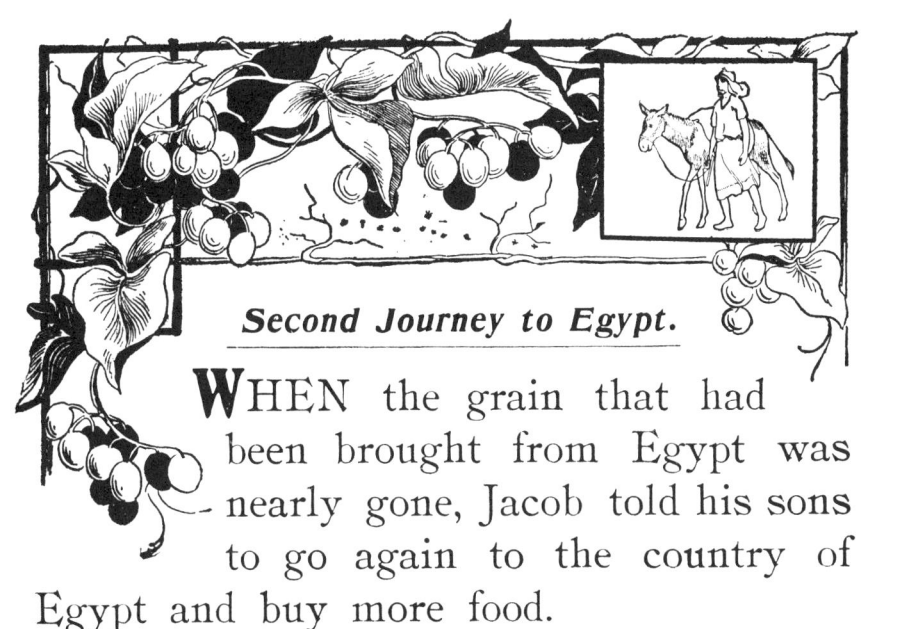

WHEN the grain that had been brought from Egypt was nearly gone, Jacob told his sons to go again to the country of Egypt and buy more food.

But Judah reminded his father that the governor of Egypt had told them not to come again unless they brought their younger brother Benjamin with them.

It was a long time before Jacob would consent to let Benjamin go. He said that Joseph was dead, Simeon was in prison in Egypt, and he feared some harm would come to Benjamin if he should go with his brothers.

But their food was almost gone, and

40 THE STORY OF JOSEPH.

all would soon die of hunger unless they should at once go to Egypt for more.

So Jacob was compelled to let Benjamin go with his brothers. And he sent by them a present to the governor of Egypt, of "a little balm, and a little honey, spices, and myrrh, nuts, and almonds."

JACOB SENDING BENJAMIN TO EGYPT.

It was not much that Jacob could send, for the famine was very severe in Canaan, where he lived.

He alse sent double money for the corn they were to buy, to make up for the money returned in their sacks before.

It was with trembling that Jacob sent his sons on this second journey to Egypt. And he said:

"God Almighty give you mercy before the man, that he may send away your other brother, and Benjamin. If I be bereaved of my children, I am bereaved."

Jacob did not know that the great governor of Egypt, whom they feared so much, was the long-lost Joseph whom he had mourned as dead for so many years.

When the men reached Egypt, and Joseph saw Benjamin with them, he told the steward of his house to bring them to his own home, and prepare a great dinner; "for these men shall dine with me at noon," he said.

The men were very much afraid when they were brought to the governor's house. They thought they were all to be made slaves because of the money that had been returned in their sacks at their first visit.

In fear they went to the steward, and talked with him about it. They told him how they had come to buy corn, and that they had paid for it. But when they opened their sacks, behold, the money they had paid was in each man's sack.

But the steward was a kind man, and told them not to fear. He said, "Peace be with you." He told them that he had had the money they paid, and that he himself had put it in their sacks.

Then he went to the prison, and got Simeon, and brought him out to them. And so they were comforted, and prepared themselves to eat with the governor.

When Joseph came to his house, they bowed down to him to the earth, and gave him the presents which their father had sent.

And he asked them of their welfare,

SECOND JOURNEY TO EGYPT.

and said, "Is your father well, the old man of whom ye spake? Is he yet alive?"

How he wanted to hear of the father he loved so well! And they answered:

"Thy servant our father is in good health, he is yet alive."

And again the brothers bowed to Joseph. When he saw his brother Benjamin, his own mother's son, he longed to embrace him, but he restrained himself, and asked:

"Is this your younger brother, of whom ye spake unto me?" And he said to Benjamin, "God be gracious unto thee, my son."

BENJAMIN.

Joseph's love for his brothers had not diminished; and when he saw them all, and Benjamin with them, his feelings overcame him, and he went into another room and wept.

The Dinner

SECOND JOURNEY TO EGYPT.

When he came to them again, he ordered the food to be brought. Then beginning with the eldest, he seated them at table according to their ages. They were much surprised to see that he knew their ages.

Joseph was seated at a table by himself, because the Egyptians considered it an abomination to eat with those who were shepherds, and Jacob's sons were all shepherds. As ruler of Egypt, Joseph must obey the customs of Egypt.

And he sent a portion of food from his own table to each of them. But to Benjamin he sent five times as much as to the others.

He wanted to know if they were jealous, as they used to be. But now they had no envy in their hearts. And they all ate and drank and were happy together.

The Silver Cup.

AFTER the dinner was finished, Joseph told the steward to fill his brothers' sacks with corn.

He also told him to put every man's money in his sack, as had been done before, and to put his silver drinking cup into Benjamin's sack.

Joseph wanted to prove his brothers once more to see if there was any selfishness remaining in them. If they were true under this test, he would be sure that they were now good and noble men.

The next morning, as soon as it was light, the men started on their long journey to their home in Canaan.

But when they had gone a little way

out of the city, Joseph sent his steward after them, to say to them:---

"Wherefore have ye rewarded evil for good?" His master had treated them well, and now they had shown their ingratitude by stealing his silver drinking cup.

But they all denied taking the cup. And they were so sure they did not have it that they promised the steward that if the cup was found with any one of them, he should die, and the rest would be slaves to the governor.

But the steward replied that only the one with whom the cup was found should be a slave to the governor, and the rest should go free.

"Then they speedily took down every man his sack to the ground, and opened every man his sack.

"And he searched, and began at the eldest, and left at the youngest; and the cup was found in Benjamin's sack."

What will these brothers do in this

calamity? A few years before they had sold one of their brothers, just for spite.

FINDING THE CUP IN BENJAMIN'S SACK.

If they return to the city with Benjamin, they put their own lives in danger. They can go free if they wish, and leave Benjamin to suffer alone.

But they are changed men, and love their brother too well to leave him in his trouble. They will not believe that Benjamin is a thief. They are sure there is a mistake somewhere.

THE SILVER CUP. 49

Then they rent their clothes, and loaded their sacks of corn upon their beasts, and returned with the steward to the city.

"And Judah and his brethren came to Joseph's house; for he was yet there: and they fell before him on the ground."

And Joseph said, "What deed is this that ye have done?" He told them they should have known that they could not deceive him.

"AND FELL BEFORE HIM ON THE GROUND."

Then Judah said, "What shall we say unto my lord? what shall we speak? or how shall we clear ourselves?" He felt the case was hopeless. The evidence was too strong to be broken; but how could he prove that Benjamin was innocent? He felt that the judgment of God for their sin in selling Joseph was now coming upon them.

So he said, "We are my lord's servant's, both we, and he also with whom the cup is found." The brothers will share the fate of Benjamin. They will not return to their father without him.

But Joseph answered, "God forbid that I should do so: but the man in whose hand the cup is found, he shall be my servant; and as for you, get you up in peace unto your father."

Judah's Reply to Joseph.

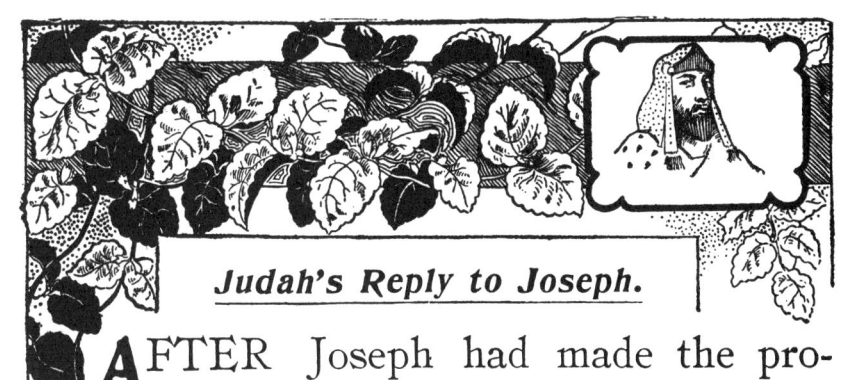

AFTER Joseph had made the proposition to hold Benjamin as a slave, and let all the rest go free, Judah stepped up close to Joseph, and said:

"O my lord, let thy servant, I pray thee, speak a word in my lord's ears, and let not thine anger burn against thy servant: for thou art even as Pharaoh.

"My lord asked his servants, saying, Have ye a father, or a brother?

"And we said unto my lord, We have a father, an old man, and a child of his old age, a little one; and his brother is dead, and he alone is left of his mother, and his father loveth him.

"And thou saidst unto thy servants,

THE STORY OF JOSEPH.

Bring him down unto me, that I may set mine eyes upon him.

"And we said unto my lord, The lad cannot leave his father: for if he should leave his father, his father would die.

"JUDAH WENT NEAR TO JOSEPH, AND SAID."

"And thou saidst unto thy servants, Except your youngest brother come down with you, ye shall see my face no more.

"And it came to pass when we came up unto thy servant my father, we told him the words of my lord.

"And our father said, Go again, and buy us a little food.

JUDAH'S REPLY TO JOSEPH.

"And we said, We cannot go down: if our youngest brother be with us, then we will go down: for we may not see the man's face, except our youngest brother be with us.

"And thy servant my father said unto us, Ye know that my wife bare me two sons:

"And the one went out from me, and I said, Surely he is torn in pieces; and I saw him not since:

"And if ye take this also from me, and mischief befall him, ye shall bring down my gray hairs with sorrow to the grave.

"Now therefore when I come to thy servant my father, and the lad be not with us; seeing that his life is bound up in the lad's life;

"It shall come to pass, when he seeth that the lad is not with us, that he will die: and thy servants shall bring down the gray hairs of thy servant our father with sorrow to the grave.

"For thy servant became surety for the lad unto my father, saying, If I bring him not unto thee, then I shall bear the blame to my father for ever.

"Now therefore, I pray thee, let thy servant abide instead of the lad a bondman to my lord; and let the lad go up with his brethren.

"For how shall I go up to my father, and the lad be not with me? lest peradventure I see the evil that shall come on my father."

Joseph Makes Himself Known

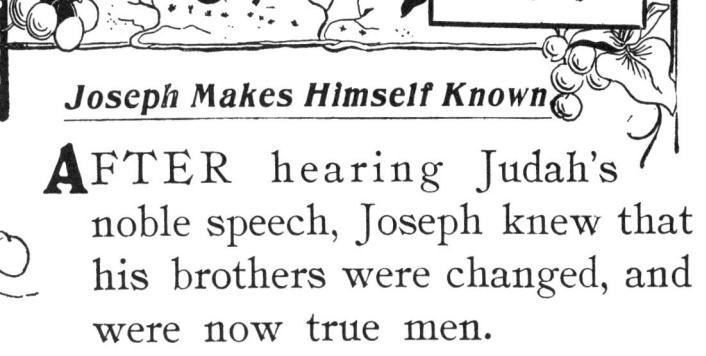

AFTER hearing Judah's noble speech, Joseph knew that his brothers were changed, and were now true men.

Then Joseph could not refrain himself any longer. So he sent all his servants from the room. And he wept aloud, and said:

"I am Joseph; doth my father yet live? And his brothers could not answer him; for they were troubled at his presence.

"And Joseph said unto his brethren, Come near unto me, I pray you. And they came near. And he said, I am Joseph your brother, whom ye sold into Egypt.

JOSEPH, 55.

"I am Joseph"

"Now therefore be not grieved, nor angry with yourselves, that ye sold me hither: for God did send me before you to preserve life."

The brothers were very much afraid when they learned that the great governor of Egypt was their brother Joseph, whom they had treated so badly many years before.

But Joseph told them not to fear; for it was God who had sent him to Egypt, and had so wonderfully prospered him.

He said to them, "Haste ye, and go up to my father, and say unto him, Thus saith thy son Joseph, God hath made me lord of all Egypt; come down unto me, tarry not."

He told them there would be still five years of famine; and if they would hasten down, he would give them the good land of Goshen as their home.

And Joseph said, "Ye shall tell my father of all my glory in Egypt, and of all that ye have seen; and ye shall haste and bring down my father hither."

Then he wept on the neck of Benjamin and of his other brothers; and after that he talked with them about his father and his home in Canaan.

When king Pharaoh learned that Joseph's brothers were with him, it pleased him well. And the king sent for Joseph, and said to him:

"Say unto thy brethren, This do ye; lade your beasts, and go, get you unto the land of Canaan; and take your father and your households, and come unto me: and I will give you the good of the land of Egypt, and ye shall eat the fat of the land.

"Now thou art commanded, this do ye; take you wagons out of the land of Egypt for your little ones, and for your wives, and bring your father, and come. Also regard not your stuff; for the good of all the land of Egypt is yours.

JOSEPH MAKES HIMSELF KNOWN.

"And the children of Israel did so: and Joseph gave them wagons, according to the commandment of Pharaoh, and gave them provision for the way." So he sent his brethren away, and they departed.

"AND JOSEPH GAVE THEM WAGONS."

And Joseph said to his brothers, "See that ye fall not out by the way." He remembered the wrong they had done him, and he wanted them to be very careful that there should not be any trouble among themselves.

Jacob Goes to Egypt.

JOSEPH'S brethren returned to their father in Canaan, and said to him, "Joseph is yet alive, and he is governor over all the land of Egypt."

Jacob could not believe the good news; but when he saw the wagons which Joseph had sent, he was glad, and said:

"It is enough; Joseph my son is yet alive: I will go and see him before I die."

Now there were seventy persons in the family of Jacob, and they took their journey with all they had, and came to Goshen in the land of Egypt.

And Joseph took his chariot and went out to meet his father at Goshen. "And he fell on his neck, and wept on his neck a good while."

JOSEPP, 60.

JACOB GOES TO EGYPT. 61

Jacob was so glad to meet Joseph, his long-lost son, that he said, "Now let me die, since I have seen thy face, because thou art yet alive." And the hearts of all were filled with joy.

"AND JOSEPH TOOK HIS CHARIOT AND WENT OUT TO MEET HIS FATHER."

Then Joseph told Pharaoh that his father and his brothers had come. And he took five of his brethren and presented them to the king.

And Pharaoh said to them, "What

JOSEPH MEETS HIS FATHER

JACOB GOES TO EGYPT.

is your occupation?" They answered, "Thy servants are shepherds."

And the king said to Joseph, "The land of Egypt is before thee; in the best of the land make thy father and brethren to dwell:

"And if thou knowest any men of activity among them, then make them rulers over my cattle. And Joseph brought in Jacob his father, and set him before Pharaoh: and Jacob blessed Pharaoh."

JACOB BLESSING PHARAOH.

And Joseph brought in his father, and presented him to the king. And Pharaoh asked Jacob, "How old art thou?

"And Jacob said unto Pharaoh, The days of the years of my pilgrimage are an hundred and thirty years: few and evil have the days of the years of my life been, and have not attained unto the days of the years of the life of my fathers in the days of their pilgrimage.

"And Jacob blessed Pharaoh and went out from before Pharaoh."

So Jacob and his sons went to the beautiful land of Goshen. and there they lived for a long time.

And Joseph cared for his father and brethren through all the years of the famine. And the children of Jacob lived in the land of Egypt many years.